The New Ibis R

Book One

by Olly N. Stanford

and Esmee E. Mejias

Illustrated by Lisa Kopper

Note to the teacher

This is the second book in the Scheme and the first full reading book. In this new edition the 30 words from the *Introductory Reader*, as well as the 78 new words, are used in somewhat different but familiar situations. This is done to accommodate 32 pages instead of the former 48 pages. These situations in which characters of familiar ethnic groups are depicted are designed to further conversation and to enlarge the pupils' reading vocabulary.

The 108 words used in this Reader are each repeated several times in a total of well over 2000 reading words. A Word List of the 78 new words is given on Page 31. A change in number is introduced by the addition of s to some of the new words, for example, "book", "books"; "kite", "kites"; "they like", "he likes". Sentences are kept short at first but longer sentences are introduced gradually later in the text. As in the *Introductory Reader* the full stop, the comma and the question mark are the punctuation marks used. Phonic work is now introduced, so that the pupils can develop confidence in tackling new words and learning to spell.

The Reader is divided into five units of stories with some revision work at the end of each unit called "Have fun with this". From Unit 2 revision lessons are followed by "Work to do" exercises. Simple instructions are provided in italics. Some of these words will not have yet been used in the Reading Scheme. The teacher should read these aloud to pupils until they begin to recognize the words and can read them for themselves. In the exercises the missing words *only* should be written. This should be done in the pupil's own Note Book and *not* in the textbook. To help pupils find the correct word each missing letter is represented by one dash.

New words should be revised frequently through the use of flashcards, the blackboard and Art and Craft lessons. A new lesson should be started only after pupils are able to recognize the words of the previous lesson readily, read the short phrases or sentences and copy or draw the shapes.

The notes to the teacher at the beginning of the Workbook or Practice Book for this Reader and the instructions at the bottom of each page must be studied carefully by the teacher.

The phonics programme

In this Scheme phonic work is introduced by guiding the pupils to recognize and learn the initial consonant sounds and the initial short vowel sounds of the words they know. Later, the short vowel sounds are combined with consonants to form final blends, for example, *an, et, op, it*. The teacher should then give practice in placing consonant sounds before these blends in order to form single syllable words, for example, *at, bat, cat; op, hop, top*. On Page 30, under the heading "Words I can make" some of these blends are shown with different initial consonants to encourage pupils to make new meaningful single syllable words.

All the letters of the alphabet except q, x and z appear in the *Introductory Book* and *Book One*. Apart from these and the letter v which is used in the words "David" and "have" all the other letters appear as initial sounds. On Page 29 these letters are printed in colour so that they may be recognized more easily by the pupils – by the shape and in most cases by sound.

2

Letter names and sounds

Pupils should be given the shapes of the letters, both capital and small, as matching exercises.

c	caocec

T	ETLTFT

After the pupils have completed two or three units of this book, most of them should be able to recognize a sufficient number of "Look and Say" words, from the text and other story books, their own names, labels on pictures, and on items in the classroom. They can now begin the simple exercise of matching the initial letter shapes of the words they know and recognizing that the sounds of the matched shapes are similar. Blackboard work and the use of matching cards are most important at this stage. Letters that have the same shape for the capital as for the small may be taught first, e.g., Cc, Pp, Ss etc., before Aa, Dd, Gg. The name and the sound of each letter should be given. Collecting words with the same initial letter shape and sound may now be played as a game and these words can be written by the pupils in their Word Books.

Word Books

A large class Word Book may be kept and after each lesson the flashcards used can be placed in slots on the correct letter page. To make individual Word Books the teacher will write each letter of the alphabet on a separate page in alphabetical order, using both the capital and small letter (Page 1 Aa, Page 2 Bb, etc.) With proper guidance and practice the pupils will be able to copy the new words they learn or the "Words I know" on the correct page in their Word Books and have fun doing it. This type of exercise is invaluable, as it will develop an understanding of dictionary skills.

3

Rags

Rags, Rags.
Come here, Rags.
Come here to me.

Look, Rags, look.
Rags, go and get it.
Get it, Rags, get it.
Go on, Rags, go on.

Come and play

Come and play, Carol.
Come and play.
I have a ball.
I have a big ball.
Let us play with this ball.
It is fun to play with a big ball.

Mummy

Look Peter, Mummy is here.
Let us go to help Mummy.
Let us help with the big bag.

No, no Rags, get down.
Get down, Rags.
Come on Peter, help me.
Help me with my big bag.

Have fun with this

Peter can play with Rags.
Come on Rags, get down.
Play with the ball.

Peter and Carol have a ball.
It is a big ball.

Carol and Peter go out with Mummy.
Peter will help Mummy with the bag.

Here Rags, come to me.
You can have this.
Have fun with it.

At play

David has come to play with Peter.
David has a bat and a ball.
The ball is not big.
The bat is not big.
Look, I have a ball, David.
You have a big ball, Peter.
My ball is not big.
Let us play with my ball.

The ball is lost

Peter hit the ball with the bat.
David can run to get the ball.
He can not find the ball.

See now you have lost my ball.
I can not find it.
Come and help me to find it.
Look, the ball is here.
The ball is not lost.

9

Work

Daddy is here.
Come, Peter and Carol,
We have work to do now.
Carol, you go and help Mummy.
Peter, come and help me here.

Indra has come.
We can not play now, Indra.
We have work to do.

Can I work with you?
I like to help.

A kitten for Carol

Daddy has come home.
He has a box.
It is a big box.
A kitten is in the box.
The kitten is for Carol.

Peter and Carol play with the kitten.
Let the kitten have the ball.
It will run and have fun with it.
A kitten likes to play with a ball.

Have fun with this

David and Peter play bat and ball.
David will hit the ball.
Is the ball lost?
Rags will help to find it.

Carol, my Daddy has a big box.
He will let you have it for the kitten.
You will like it.

Carol and Indra have fun with the kitten.

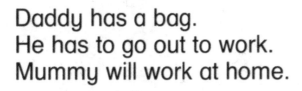

The kitten will not come down.
No Rags, do not go in.
This box is not for you.

Daddy has a bag.
He has to go out to work.
Mummy will work at home.

Work to do

Fill in the names.
The pictures will help you.
Write the words in your Note Book.

1. D – – – – has come to play with Peter.
2. P – – – – has lost the ball.
3. R – – – has the ball.
4. I – – – – will play with Carol.
5. Peter will help M – – – – with the bag.
6. D – – – – has a kitten.
7. The kitten is for C – – – –.

The supermarket

Mummy, Carol and Peter are at the
supermarket.
Peter and Carol like to go to the
supermarket.
Do we want milk, Mummy?
Yes Carol, we want milk.
Will you get it?
You and Peter like to drink milk.

Look at this, Peter.
Do you like it?
We can get this for Daddy.
He will like it.

The toy shop and book store

Peter and Carol are
at the toy shop.
They look at the toys.
Carol likes the big doll.
Peter looks at the bats.
Mummy will get a doll for Carol
and a bat for Peter.

At the book store Peter looks
at the books.
Peter has a book and Carol likes it.
Mummy can I have this book?
Mummy gets it for Carol.
I will get this book for you, Peter.

At the bus stop

We have to go home now.
Let us go to the bus stop.
Look Mummy, David is at the bus stop.
Can we go with him?
No Peter, we take this bus.
That bus will not take us home.
Come, get in this bus.

The bus will stop here.
Mummy, Peter and Carol get
out of the bus.
Peter and Carol run to get home.
Daddy will like to look at the books.

Have fun with this

David and Peter are at the supermarket.
David wants to get milk to drink.
David likes a drink of milk.
Do you?

The bus will take Indra to the toy shop.
Will that shop have books and dolls?
Indra will go in to find out.

Daddy and Carol want to go to the supermarket.
Daddy stops the bus and he and Carol get in.
The bus will stop at the supermarket.
Daddy and Carol will get out of the bus.

Mummy and Peter are
in the book store.
Peter wants that book.
Will Mummy get it for him?

supermarket drink take store toy bus milk stop doll book

Work to do

Fill in the missing letters to make words.
The words on the bus will help you.
Write them in your Note Book.

1. A s————————— is a big shop.
2. Carol likes a d———— of milk.
3. S——— that bus, David.
4. I can get a b——— at the store.
5. We t——— this bus to go home.
6. I will get m——— for the kitten.
7. We can get toys at that s————.
8. You can play with my d———, Carol.
9. Here is the b—— stop.
10. Indra will get a doll at the t—— shop.

A birthday party

This is a party for Joy.
It is a birthday party.
Carol has come to the party.
Carol has a book for Joy.
Peter, David and Indra are at the
birthday party.
What do they have?
They have a toy, a book and a doll for Joy.
They play and have fun.

Help for David

Peter has a kite.
David has a kite.
My kite will not go up, Peter.
Let me see the kite, David.
Let me help you.
The kite will need a tail at this end.
A tail at this end will help it to go up.

See David with the kite.
It can go up now.
He can have fun with it.
Can you make a kite?

Skip and play

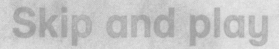

Carol, Indra and Joy skip.
David and Peter come to see.
Can we play with you?
Yes, you can play with us.
David can not skip.
Peter can not skip.
Let us help you.

Take this end, David.
Peter, now jump with me.
Jump, one, two, three.
Yes, you can do it, you can skip.

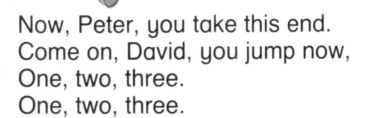

Now, Peter, you take this end.
Come on, David, you jump now,
One, two, three.
One, two, three.

21

Have fun with this

Joy, Carol and Indra are at a party.
It is not a birthday party.
They have fun at this party.

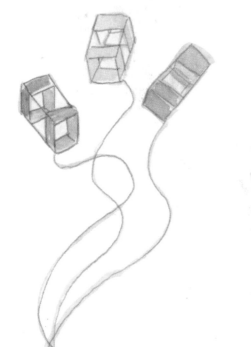

Up, up, up go the kites.
We can see one, two, three kites.
They do not need tails now.
Can David make a kite?
Yes, he can make one.

Peter wants to skip.
He will need David and Joy to help him.
You take that end, David.
Jump Peter, one, two, three.

Work to do

Can you find the missing words?
The words on the kites will help you.
Write them in your Note Book.

1. Here is a big ————.
2. Joy and Carol ————.
3. Rags can sit ——.
4. We can go to a —————.
5. Can you see his ————?
6. The kite has a tail on this ———.
7. ——— can play with Rags.
8. Rags likes to ———— on Carol.
9. I have ——— kittens.
10. Jump one, two, —————, Peter.

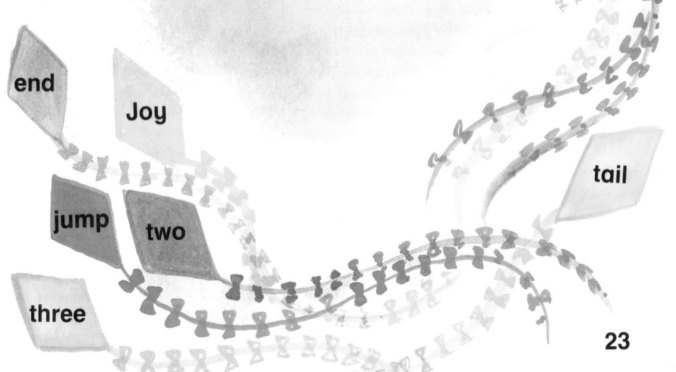

kite

skip up

party

end

Joy

jump two

three

tail

Pets

See David with his pet dog.
It is a big dog.
David will run and jump with his pet dog.
A big dog needs to run and jump.
David has a bone for his pet dog.
What will the big dog do with it?

A kitten can not eat a bone.
Carol will put milk for the kitten.
A kitten needs milk.
What will Peter get for his pet dog, Rags?
Peter will get a bone for him.

24

The big cat

Can you see Indra?
Yes, Indra has a pet cat.
The cat likes to sit by Indra.
The cat has three kittens.
One little kitten sits by the box.
Can you see the little tail?
Two little kittens sit by the big cat.

A big cat likes to eat fish.
A little kitten needs to drink milk.
Indra will put fish for the cat.
The kittens will get milk.

A pet rabbit

The little rabbit can hop, hop, hop.
It is a pet rabbit.
Joy and Carol play with the pet rabbit.
They have fun.

Do you like my rabbit, Carol?
Yes I do.
Can I get a rabbit, Joy?
Yes Carol, my Daddy
can get one for you.

It is time for me to go home.
I will have to run now.
I can not get wet.

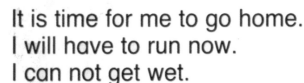

Joy, where is the rabbit?
Do not let it get wet.
What will Joy do?

It is time to eat.
Peter likes to eat fish.
This time he gets a bone in his fish.
He needs to take the bone out.

The little pet rabbit will go hop, hop, hop.
Where will it go now?
Do not let it go out.
Do not let it get lost.

Stop that, Peter, stop that.
We do not want to get wet.
Put that down, put it down.
Run Carol, run.

Where is my pet cat?
It sits by the big dog.
The pet cat likes to play with my big dog.

Work to do

Can you find the missing words?
Write them in your Note Book.
The words on the fish will help you.

1. Peter gets a ———— in his fish.
2. Carol wants a pet ——————.
3. Joy and Carol do not like to get ———.
4. It is ———— to eat.
5. A rabbit can ———.
6. A ——— can eat a bone.
7. A cat will eat ————.
8. The pet cat will ——— by the dog.
9. Mummy will ——— milk for the kitten.
10. Do you like to ——— fish?
11. —————— is the rabbit?
12. A kitten is a —————— cat.

bone   rabbit   wet   time   hop
dog   fish   sit   get   eat   where
little

Words I know

Words that appear in the *Introductory Book* are shown with asterisks.

Aa
a*
and*
at*
are

Bb
ball*
bag
bat
big
birthday
book
bone
box
bus
by

Cc
can*
Carol*
cat
come*

Dd
Daddy
David
do
dog
doll
down
drink

Ee
eat
end

Ff
find
fish
for
fun

Gg
get*
go

Hh
has
have
he
help
here*
him
his
hit
hop
home

Ii
I*
in*
Indra*
it*
is*

Jj
Joy
jump

Kk
kite
kitten

Ll
let*
like
little
look*
lost

Mm
make
me*
milk
Mummy
my*

Nn
needs
no*
not
now*

Oo
of
on
one
out*

Pp
party
pet
Peter*
play*
put

Rr
rabbit
Rags
run*

Ss
see*
shop
sit
skip
stop
store
supermarket

Tt
take
tail
that
the*
they
this
three
time
to
toy
two

Uu
up
us*

Ww
want
we
wet
what
where
will*
with*
work

Yy
yes
you*

Words I can make

A at	E et	I it	O ot	U un
bat	let	sit	pot	bun
cat	met	lit	lot	sun
fat	wet	hit	hot	fun
sat	get	bit	got	gun
	pet			run

an	en	in	op	ut
fan	men	bin	hop	cut
man	ten	pin	mop	hut
pan	hen	tin	top	nut
van	pen	win	pop	but

ap	ed	ill	oy	um
cap	bed	will	boy	sum
map	red	pill	toy	gum
lap	fed	hill	Joy	hum
tap	led	fill	Roy	

end	ig
bend	fig
lend	dig
send	pig
mend	big

Word list

The 78 new words used in *Book One* appear in the following order.

p.4	Rags	p.10	work		doll		two
	to		Daddy	p.16	bus		three
	go		we		stop	p.24	pets
	on		do		him		his
p.5	have		like		take		dog
	big	p.11	kitten		that		bone
	this		home		of		eat
	fun		box	p.19	birthday		put
p.6	Mummy		for		party	p.25	cat
	help	p.14	super-		Joy		sit
	bag		market		what		by
	down		are	p.20	kite		little
p.8	David		want		up		fish
	has		milk		need	p.26	rabbit
	bat		drink		tail		hop
	not	p.15	toy		end		time
p.9	lost		shop		make		wet
	hit		book	p.21	skip		where
	he		store		yes		
	find		they		jump		
					one		

Numbers

first second third fourth

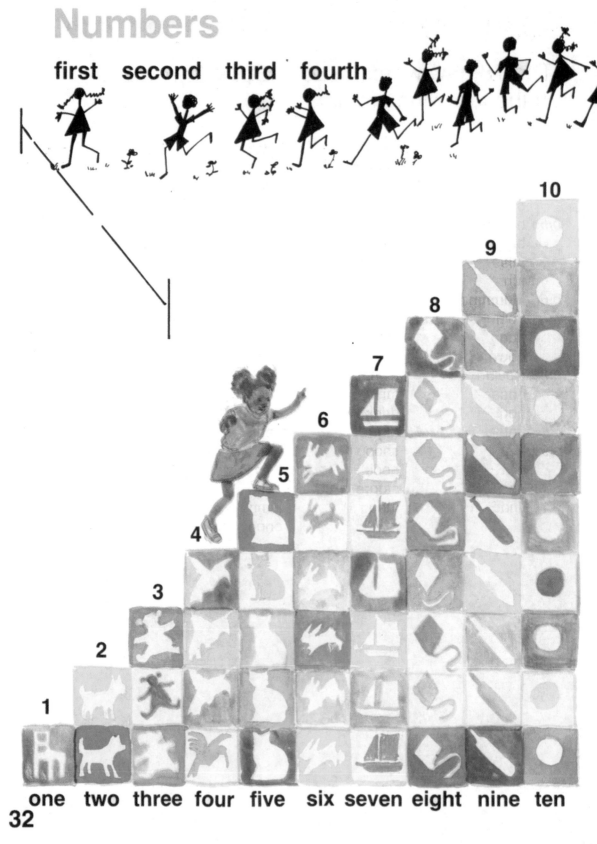

one   two   three   four   five   six   seven   eight   nine   ten

1 2 3 4 5 6 7 8 9 10

The Giant Turtle